P

Barnabas

SON OF ENCOURAGEMENT

CWR

Christopher Brearley

For list of National Distributors, visit www.cwr.org.uk/distributors

Unless otherwise indicated, all Scripture references are from the Holy Bible: New International Version (NIV), copyright © 1973, 1978, 1984 by the International Bible Society.
Other versions used: NKJV: *New King James Version*, © 1982, Thomas Nelson Inc.

Concept development, editing, design and production by CWR
Printed in the UK by Linney.

ISBN: 978-1-85345-911-5

Contents

Introduction

Of all the leaders in the Early Church few, if any, were as humble as and more heroic than Barnabas. Within Acts are scattered several passages that describe his usefulness as a Christian. Paul, also, refers to him in his first letter to the Corinthians (9:6); Galatians (2:1,9,13) and Colossians (4:10).

Barnabas is remembered primarily for one thing: wherever he went he encouraged people and enabled them to have a much closer walk with God. He did not give up on people when they made a mistake. What would have happened to Paul (also called Saul – his Hebrew name which I use at times in these studies), John Mark, and numerous others, had it not been for the forgiveness and help of Barnabas? He put the interests of others before his own.

During the course of history some great things have occurred that might not have done so were it not for the work of a much lesser-known person. One instance of this is Martin Luther's conversion and the huge changes he precipitated through the Protestant Reformation. But the part played by his sensitive superior at the monastery, Johann von Staupitz, is usually forgotten. With shrewd insight and under the guidance of the Holy Spirit, von Staupitz helped Luther to experience the loving forgiveness of God through Jesus Christ. What would have happened to Luther had it not been for the help and encouragement of his superior?

Most people don't like to be excelled by someone else. It is difficult for any of us to truthfully say, 'I must decrease and he or she must increase.' Barnabas, however, was willing to play a secondary role to that of Paul. He didn't allow divisive worldly thoughts and competitiveness to influence him to advance his own reputation. His sole ambition was to do great things for God and give Him the glory.

Barnabas practised what he preached and so gave generously to those in genuine need. He not only sacrificed his possessions but also his time and energy so that the Church might flourish. He experienced suffering and readily risked his life for the sake of the Lord Jesus Christ: 'He was a good man, full of the Holy Spirit and faith ...' (Acts 11:24). No better statement could be accorded any Christian.

Was Barnabas a perfect man? No, he wasn't. He was human just like us (Acts 14:15). Even the best person has faults and falls short of God's glorious standard. So God reveals the life story of someone like Barnabas to show us what He can do, by the power of His Spirit, through ordinary men and women who have faith in Him. Barnabas, despite his failings, was used mightily by God to influence the course of church history.

Barnabas was a Levite and was born on Cyprus (Acts 4:36), a beautiful island in the eastern part of the Mediterranean Sea, where there lived a large Jewish colony in the first century AD. Thus he was a foreign-born Jew. We are not told why he came to Jerusalem. Perhaps it was because his cousin John Mark and Aunt Mary lived there. Because he was a Levite (ie of the tribe of Levi) he was entitled to perform minor duties in the Temple. Levites stood midway between the people and the priests who, although themselves were Levites, claimed particular descent from Aaron, a grandson of Levi. The fact that Barnabas was a Levite reveals that not all those associated with the Temple were inexorable enemies of the gospel.

The Bible does not tell us when or how Barnabas died although several legends attempt to do so. Obviously such knowledge is irrelevant. All that we need to know is that Barnabas had a great influence for good on many Christians through his life. Why did he do the things that he did? Are they still relevant for us today? Yes, they certainly are! God has a plan for each one of us that may be very different to what we expect. How do we respond to God's call? Barnabas faced many of the challenges that we face now. What can we learn from him that will help strengthen our faith and increase our ability to help others to put their trust in God?

There is a tremendous need for the ministry of encouragement in today's Church. I know that there have been difficult times when I needed to be encouraged. And there have also been times when God used me to be an encouragement to others. All God's people will at some point in life face difficulties, and the strength that comes from compassion and encouragement is essential. Occasionally just a smile is a great encouragement (see Job 29:24). Similarly a little kindness can often be a tremendous help to a Christian in difficult circumstances. We urgently need men and women who, guided by the Holy Spirit, will encourage believers in the same way that Barnabas the 'Son of Encouragement' did. Are we like Barnabas? Are we willing to help others, and patiently work with them so that they can become the very best they can be in the Lord? If we do, the world will be a better place.

WEEK 1

Helping the Needy

Opening Icebreaker

Discuss what simple acts of kindness you might do to help others as a demonstration of your Christian faith.

Bible Readings

- Acts 4:32–37
- 1 John 3:17–20
- 2 Corinthians 9:7

Opening Our Eyes

Genuine love will inevitably lead to kindness and help in deed as well as word. Hence, members of the Jerusalem church who owned land or houses sold them and brought the money to the apostles to give to others who lacked the basic necessities of life (Acts 4:34–35). Does this incident teach that all Spirit-filled believers should sell their personal property, establish a common fund, and share the proceeds? No, that is a Marxist, not a Christian, doctrine. A person might say, 'What I possess is not my own.' But nobody said, 'What you possess is ours.' The generosity of these Christians in Jerusalem resulted not from coercive ideology but because of their extraordinary unity of heart and soul. It was an utterly spontaneous and voluntary gesture that outwardly expressed the love and solidarity of the Jerusalem church. From time to time, as genuine needs arose, the wealthy sold possessions adequate to alleviate the suffering of others.

Having described the sacrificial giving of the Jerusalem church, Luke supplies us with a specific example of a man called Joses, or Joseph, who was also named Barnabas by the apostles (Acts 4:36). Barnabas was not unique in selling property to support those in urgent need. There were many other people who did likewise. Why mention Barnabas? Probably he was singled out by Luke because of his future leadership role and also the fact that he set a fine example for others to follow. He was a man whose deeds matched his words. Barnabas was immensely grateful for what God had done for him and showed his appreciation by sacrificing one of his possessions. He sold a field that he owned and brought the money to the apostles for redistribution to those in need. There is no evidence to suggest that he sold all of his property, thus becoming poor himself. Even so, this in no way nullifies the truth that he gave sacrificially out of a grateful heart.

Barnabas was moved by the Holy Spirit to do what he did. As a result his selflessness and sacrifice received much praise and thanksgiving among the many believers. When Ananias and Sapphira, husband and wife, saw this they were envious and wanted similar recognition for themselves. Their decision to sell some property paralleled that of Barnabas with one major difference. They gave only part of the money to the apostles, but claimed it was the full amount. Ananias and Sapphira were motivated by a completely different spirit than that of Barnabas (Acts 5:3). Their hypocrisy was an attempt to make people think more highly of them than they knew was deserved. They wanted the credit for sacrificial giving without making the sacrifice. By their selfish and sacrilegious behaviour they were denying a fundamental truth of the Christian faith, that is, we should not give in order to get. In addition the sin of Ananias and Sapphira, like all sin, is finally not against human beings but against God (Acts 5:4).

The conversion of Barnabas to Christianity and his Christlikeness must have been a tremendous encouragement to the apostles. His greatest desire was to please God and that motivated him to help others. Because of his faith in Christ he gave willingly to those in need so that God would be glorified. This generous act of sharing within the Early Church is the first reference to Barnabas that we have.

Discussion Starters

1. Why is it incorrect to say that it was the standard practice of the Early Christians to totally liquidate their assets in order to distribute to the poor?

_____

_____

_____

_____

_____

2. How do the actions of Ananias and Sapphira (Acts 5:1–11) differ from those of Barnabas? What lessons do we learn from each of them?

_____

_____

_____

_____

_____

3. When was the last time you expressed your thanks and appreciation to those who have been a blessing to you?

_____

_____

_____

_____

_____

4. Read 2 Corinthians 9:6–15 and discuss the principles of generous giving.

_____

_____

_____

_____

_____

5. Read James 2:14–26. Why do you think it is said that faith without works and conversely works without faith do not result in salvation?

_____

_____

_____

_____

_____

6. Some people are lonely today because, unlike Barnabas, they build barriers instead of bridges. Why is healthy fellowship essential?

_____

_____

_____

_____

_____

7. Why do Christians get discouraged? How might we find or give encouragement in the midst of problems?

_____

_____

_____

_____

_____

8. What level of support and accountability should a local fellowship of believers have toward each other?

_____

_____

_____

_____

_____

Personal Application

People have various attitudes towards possessions. They might selfishly say, 'What's mine is mine.' Or, even worse, 'What's yours is mine.' Those who are very generous will say, 'What's mine is yours.' Which of these do you consider to be the correct attitude? The answer is none of them. The Bible clearly teaches that what is mine is His (1 Chron. 29:14). Everything that a person possesses is given by God and so it should be used for His glory. Barnabas believed this and therefore readily responded to God's goodness with great gratitude and generosity.

God gives us numerous things that we do not deserve. Consequently, like Barnabas, all Christians should be grateful and unreservedly show it by their generosity. Anyone who is truly thankful for God's abounding grace will show Him gratitude by being a generous giver. The primary motive will be neither self-concern nor love for others, but a deep love of God.

Seeing Jesus in the Scriptures

Jesus told the story of a man who accumulated great wealth for himself and ignored giving anything to the poor; this man was condemned by God as a fool (Luke 12:16–21). That is not to condemn riches or possessions in and of themselves. The New Testament doesn't support this. It can be good to have money and enjoy the many things that it can buy. But we should constantly remember that we have a duty to give enthusiastically and sacrificially to people in urgent need so that God will be glorified. Caring for the poor is evidence of the presence of Christ in our hearts.

WEEK 2

A True Friend

Opening Icebreaker

Abraham was called 'God's friend' (James 2:23), a title that expresses the closeness of their relationship. Identify some of the characteristics that are necessary to develop healthy relationships with others.

Bible Readings

- Genesis 2:18
- Acts 9:20–27
- Luke 17:3–4

Opening Our Eyes

From the beginning the Bible reveals that people were created as relational beings (Gen. 2:18). God wants everyone to have lasting friendships here on earth. Having said that, how does one recognise potential friends? Some people say, 'Oh, he's a true friend of mine,' yet in reality this is often a gross exaggeration. Hence, what is the mark of true friendship? The well-known proverb, 'A friend in need is a friend indeed', contains wise advice. It clearly teaches that true friendship remains intact regardless of changing external circumstances. A true friend will support you even when everyone else opposes or avoids you. A true friend stays true to the end.

Just because you are a Christian does not mean that you will never encounter problems nor need encouragement or reassurance of God's forgiveness. We all need someone we can trust and with whom we may share our deepest thoughts. Friendship is an essential part of what it means to be a Christian. It is to help each other as we walk together along the way God has laid out for us. People who are alone when they fall have no one to help them up. An ancient Jewish proverb aptly reminds us that 'A friendless man is like the left hand without the right'.

A good example of true friendship in the New Testament is that shown by Barnabas to Saul. When Saul arrived in Jerusalem he found himself in a very difficult situation. His former associates were aware of his defection and, of course, would have hated him. In their eyes he was a traitor to the cause of Judaism. He also encountered problems when he attempted to join the Jerusalem church for worship and prayer. Understandably the Christians in Jerusalem were afraid of him and suspicious of his motives. How could it be otherwise considering his past record?

Evidently they were not familiar with the story of his
miraculous conversion and of how he had preached
with power in Damascus. They thought he was only
pretending to be a believer! How were they to know that
this was not a stratagem to infiltrate the church and do
still greater damage? Could this once formidable adversary
of the Christian faith possibly have become its greatest
advocate?

Saul desperately needed someone who could serve as an
intermediary to introduce him to the Christian leaders in
Jerusalem. But who would be willing to fulfil this difficult
yet vital role of mediation? When everyone else, fearful
and uncertain, was avoiding him, Barnabas came to the
rescue. He realised Saul's need for acceptance by the
Christian Church. Barnabas saw beyond Saul's reputation;
he saw the change in his heart – a heart no longer filled
with prejudice and violent hatred. These terrible traits in
Saul had now been replaced by love and humility.

You don't have to ask a true friend for help, he or she
just gives it. Barnabas did not hold people's pasts against
them for love is always forgetful in remembering injury
and injustice. Love is patient and kind, it does not keep
a record of things said or done against us (1 Cor. 13:4–5).
Therefore, Barnabas readily introduced Saul to the
apostles and encouraged them to accept him for who he
now was. Barnabas explained to them firstly, that Saul
had seen the Lord on the way to Damascus; secondly,
what the Lord had said to Saul and, thirdly, that in the
local synagogues of Damascus he had preached boldly
in the name of Jesus. As a result of this account from
Barnabas, a witness who was respected because of his
previous record, Saul was accepted as a Christian brother.

Discussion Starters

1. Saul stood alone between Judaism and Christianity, for neither trusted him. Why was this?

   _____

   _____

   _____

   _____

   _____

2. If you had been Barnabas, how would you have felt about reaching out and accepting Saul as a dear brother in Christ?

   _____

   _____

   _____

   _____

   _____

3. Why, other than guidance by the Holy Spirit, might we expect Barnabas to help Saul?

   _____

   _____

   _____

   _____

   _____

4. Think of some biblical examples of those who showed signs of true friendship.

   _____

   _____

   _____

   _____

   _____

5. Did Barnabas take a calculated or reckless risk in acting as an intermediary for Saul? How do you support your answer?

_____

_____

_____

_____

_____

6. Barnabas was prepared to forgive people who had made serious mistakes. What implications does this have for Christians?

_____

_____

_____

_____

_____

7. Can we expect to receive God's forgiveness if we are unwilling to forgive others?

_____

_____

_____

_____

_____

8. Why was the intervention of Barnabas so important? What lessons does this have for us?

_____

_____

_____

_____

_____

Personal Application

If we love God and our neighbours we shall not fear in the sense of being alarmed or frightened. Such fear is inconsistent with love and so it will be extinguished from our hearts (1 John 4:18). For this reason Barnabas was not afraid of Saul and gladly accepted him as a brother in Christ.

Sadly, one of the common characteristics of human nature is that when some people make mistakes they are forever condemned. Some churches today are plagued by disagreements and divisions because their members are more concerned with trivial controversies than with fellowship and outreach. Alas there are many effective sons and daughters of discouragement in our midst.

Seeing Jesus in the Scriptures

Jesus said to His disciples, 'Greater love has no-one than this, that he lay down his life for his friends. You are my friends if you do what I command. I no longer call you servants, because a servant does not know his master's business. Instead, I have called you friends, for everything that I learned from my Father I have made known to you' (John 15:13–15). Jesus proved His friendship by what He said and did. Does that apply to us? How much are we prepared to sacrifice or suffer for our friends? We must be to Jesus what He is to us, and we must be to others too what He is to us.

WEEK 3

Full of the Holy Spirit and Strong in Faith

Opening Icebreaker

'Do you not know,' asks Paul, 'that your body is a temple of the Holy Spirit, who is in you, whom you have received from God?' (1 Cor. 6:19). How is this relevant for members of your group?

Bible Readings

- Acts 6:1–10
- Acts 11:19–24
- Luke 11:11–13

Opening Our Eyes

Those in the Jerusalem church heard about the many Gentile believers in Antioch and were concerned. They responded by sending someone to investigate the strange events that were happening there and to give encouragement and direction as needed. To its great credit the Jerusalem church diligently kept a close watch on developments elsewhere.

It is not possible to say whether or not Barnabas took the initiative in offering his services for this necessary mission. What is certain is that the church saw in Barnabas the required gifts to represent them. His character and abilities made him a wise choice. Being a Greek-speaking Jewish Christian and a native of Cyprus, like some of the evangelists at Antioch, he could easily identify with these believers. Barnabas was the best available ambassador for this sensitive and very important task. His mission was not to wield authority, to find fault or counsel caution, but rather to encourage and help nurture this new multicultural church.

Obviously, from what we are told, Barnabas proved himself to be the right man at the right time. 'When he came and had seen the grace of God, he was glad, and encouraged them all that with purpose of heart they should continue with the Lord' (Acts 11:23, NKJV). Barnabas strikes me as a Christian who was often glad because he was a good man, full of the Holy Spirit and of faith. He was not a dogmatic disciplinarian; rather he wholeheartedly focused on his outstanding ministry of encouragement.

Are we always glad to see the grace of God working in the lives of other Christians? Or, are we sometimes envious if their abilities appear to be much greater than our own? Do we perhaps sometimes envy the spiritual blessings experienced by other churches and think, 'Why isn't it like this in my church?' Such comparisons and competitiveness are always wrong because they interfere with human relationships and are contrary to God's standard for holiness. Therefore, let us be glad with others in their success and never wish their success were ours. Barnabas was excited by, not envious of, the success of others. When he saw what was happening in Antioch he was filled with joy, and he encouraged the believers to stay true to the Lord. He was a good man, strong in faith, who set an excellent and necessary example for them and us to follow.

The adjective 'good' used by Luke (Acts 11:24), aptly describes the personal character of Barnabas. His primary aim was to serve God and as a result he was willing to make sacrifices for the welfare of others. Barnabas had the ability to rise above narrow Jewish sectarianism because, like Stephen (Acts 6:5; 7:55), he was 'full of the Holy Spirit.'

To be filled with the Spirit means that our lives are totally available to God. Without the Spirit it is not possible to live like Christ. But controlled by the Spirit we can reproduce Christlikeness: 'love, joy, peace, longsuffering, kindness, goodness, faithfulness, gentleness, self-control' (Gal. 5:22–23, NKJV). Barnabas did not depend on his own strength; instead he had complete faith in the promises of God. He knew that with the power of the Spirit there is no problem which is ever too great.

Discussion Starters

1. The church at Antioch experienced a sudden influx of many people who were new to Christianity. What problems might this have caused?

_____

_____

_____

_____

_____

2. Why was Barnabas a wise choice to encourage the Christians at Antioch to keep on serving God?

_____

_____

_____

_____

_____

3. Barnabas 'encouraged them all' (Acts 11:23). He didn't show favouritism. What implications does this have for us today?

_____

_____

_____

_____

_____

4. The presence of Barnabas in Antioch was far more than a fleeting visit. What does this suggest?

_____

_____

_____

_____

_____

5. As soon as God begins to bless a church, Satan will surely attack. How can Christians avoid yielding to temptation?

_____

_____

_____

_____

_____

6. Is the same power of the Holy Spirit that came upon God's servants in the past available to us today?

_____

_____

_____

_____

_____

7. What characteristics would you expect to see in the life of someone who was full of the Holy Spirit?

_____

_____

_____

_____

_____

8. How should our faith in God affect the way we live?

_____

_____

_____

_____

_____

Personal Application

Because the Christian life is a supernatural life, the only way to live it is by supernatural power. All of the worthwhile activity in the formation of the church in Antioch is driven by the power of the Holy Spirit. Otherwise nothing of any lasting value could have been accomplished. Every Christian needs to be filled with the Spirit again and again (Eph. 5:18) for it is impossible to experience a once and for all fullness. That is why some of those who were filled with the Holy Spirit at Pentecost (Acts 2:4) received further outpourings to enable them to face new challenges. When the great American evangelist of the nineteenth century, Dwight L. Moody, was asked why he said that he needed to be filled continually with the Holy Spirit, he replied, 'Because I leak!' That surely applies to each one of us.

Seeing Jesus in the Scriptures

Jesus, while proclaiming Himself to be the Son of God, chose to serve rather than be served (Mark 10:45). He is the ultimate role model of a leader for us to follow. We are to be interested in others, also, and what they are doing. As the Spirit of the Lord works within us we will readily sacrifice personal time and resources for humankind without ever expecting to be repaid. Only then can we fully experience the abundant life God has for us (John 10:10).

WEEK 4

Ministering Together

Opening Icebreaker

On their missionary journey (Acts 13:1–3), Barnabas and Saul are sent out together. Discuss what you consider to be the advantages of teamwork.

Bible Readings

- Acts 11:25–30
- Acts 12:25–14:7

Opening Our Eyes

God chose to work through an individual like Barnabas
to add even more converts to the church in Antioch.
For this reason the work progressed very well under his
leadership and soon the gathering grew too large for
him to manage alone. Being full of the Holy Spirit and
of faith he realised that it was essential to find a suitable
colleague who could share this great responsibility of
teaching the Gentile Christians. Furthermore, he knew the
ideal person for this difficult role. Saul was his man and
so he would diligently search for him.

Previously Barnabas had stood by Saul and introduced
him to the Jerusalem church (Acts 9:27). He had explained
to them how Saul had been miraculously converted on
the road to Damascus. Barnabas had not forgotten this
and in all probability he was aware of, and remembered,
the words God had spoken to Ananias. 'Go, for he
[Saul] is a chosen vessel of Mine to bear my name
before Gentiles, kings, and the children of Israel' (Acts
9:15, NKJV). Moreover, Barnabas knew how Saul had
preached boldly in Damascus and Jerusalem that Jesus
was indeed the Son of God. He would undoubtedly
have been impressed by Saul's absolute commitment and
determination to proclaim the gospel message. Saul's
outstanding credentials and the Lord's leading convinced
Barnabas to now bring Saul to Antioch as quickly as
possible.

Our last encounter with Saul was seven or eight years ago
in Jerusalem – from where he had to escape by way of
Caesarea to Tarsus, his own native city. How did Barnabas
know that Saul was still in Tarsus and that his journey
there would not be a waste of time? It is not possible for
us to say. All we are told is that Barnabas left for Tarsus
to look for Saul. Neither do we know how long this
search in Tarsus and its vicinity took. Luke (the writer of

Acts) simply informs us that Barnabas found him. Can you imagine Saul's reaction when Barnabas says, 'We need you in Antioch'? How much convincing did Barnabas have to do? I believe that Saul would have been very happy to see the man who had stood by him in Jerusalem and encouraged him. Also he must surely have felt some sense of excitement when presented with the opportunity to go to a city where there were many new Gentile believers, eager to learn more about Jesus. Saul knew that he was the Lord's chosen instrument to take the gospel message to the Gentiles (Acts 22:21). This was the moment he had patiently waited for. Hence, Saul would return with Barnabas to Antioch and from there he would eventually travel throughout the ancient Mediterranean world, preaching, teaching and establishing new churches.

The humility of Barnabas in his willingness to share the ministry with Saul is admirable. He had recruited a co-worker whom he knew had an exceptional understanding of the Old Testament Scriptures and of how they had been fulfilled in Jesus Christ. Barnabas realised his own limitations and acknowledged that Saul was a much better teacher than himself. Neither did he descend to the level of being envious of another Christian. He did not compare himself to Saul nor try to compete with him in any way for personal recognition. Barnabas knew that one of the decisive tests of an encourager is the ability to let someone else take the lead and get the credit.

Discussion Starters

1. Barnabas realised his own limitations and humbly acknowledged this by asking Saul for help. How does God respond to the humble (Psa. 18:27; Matt. 23:12)?

2. How should a Christian's understanding of greatness affect his or her behaviour as a leader (Mark 9:35; John 3:30)?

3. Why is giving to both God and others necessary? How much should we give (Acts 11:29–30)?

4. Read Acts 11:27–30 and then discuss how the new Christians in Antioch demonstrated that they were true members of the family of God.

5. How was Barnabas significant in breaking down the barrier between Jews and Gentiles?

_____

_____

_____

_____

_____

6. How might Christians react when the gifts and abilities of others exceed their own? How should they?

_____

_____

_____

_____

_____

7. The church in Antioch was actively involved in commissioning Barnabas and Saul as missionaries. What is the significance of this for us?

_____

_____

_____

_____

_____

8. Good leaders, like Barnabas, look to the future. Therefore, they mentor others to ensure the continuation of God's work. How can we enable other Christians to develop their God-given gifts?

_____

_____

_____

_____

_____

Personal Application

If any church is to be successful it needs a multiplicity of gifts which no one individual can provide. Barnabas realised this and so he commendably sought appropriate help. How many Christian leaders today would do what he did? More often than not help is only requested during times of extreme difficulty but here, in Antioch, the church was experiencing great blessing. Why share the credit for this with someone else? Obviously Barnabas did not focus upon himself but readily reached out to others. His ambition and great gift was to develop teamwork. He knew that when Christians work together, they divide the effort and multiply the effect.

Seeing Jesus in the Scriptures

A brief statement by Luke informs us that it was at Antioch that the believers were first called Christians (Acts 11:26). This name appears only twice more in the New Testament, in Acts 26:28 and 1 Peter 4:16. On each occasion it is not used by Christians of themselves; it is a nickname given by their non-believing neighbours. This suggests that Christians are now becoming numerous and that they were easily distinguished from other people. The Early Christians clearly identified themselves with Christ by making Him the main topic of their conversation wherever they went. Is that the reason why we are called Christians today? Or do we often behave in a way that is virtually the same as that of our non-Christian neighbours? Jesus calls each of us to follow His example (Matt. 16:24).

WEEK 5

To God be the Glory

Opening Icebreaker

The first great commandment is: 'Love the LORD your God with all your heart and with all your soul and with all your strength' (Deut. 6:5). Consider how we might display our love for God.

Bible Readings

- Exodus 20:1–6
- Acts 12:21–23
- Revelation 22:8–9
- Acts 14:8–28

Opening Our Eyes

One day when the city of Lystra was crowded, maybe for a pagan festival, Paul saw a man who had been unable to walk from birth. This man listened intently as Paul preached the gospel of salvation, and Paul noticed him and realised that he had faith to be healed. So, Paul confidently called to this man in a loud voice, 'Stand up straight on your feet!' And the man jumped to his feet and walked for the first time in his life.

The large superstitious crowd is deeply impressed by what has happened, for nobody had ever seen such a miracle before. Surely, they thought, Barnabas and Paul must be gods who had come to earth in human form. They imagined that Barnabas was the Greek god Zeus and that Paul was Hermes.

The Roman poet Ovid, who lived from 43 BC to AD 17, wrote in his *Metamorphoses* about an ancient myth concerning a visit of Zeus and Hermes. Both Zeus, the chief of the gods, and Hermes, the messenger of the gods, had come disguised as mortal men. None of the local people would provide them with hospitality until, finally, an elderly man named Philemon and his wife Baucis welcomed the gods to their humble home. As a result the gods richly rewarded the couple's hospitality and destroyed the homes, by flood, of those who would not accommodate them.

It is likely that these Lystran people were well acquainted with this story and were determined not to suffer a similar fate. Acting on the surmise that the gods had once again taken on the likeness of men, the priest and the crowds of people wished to honour Barnabas and Saul.

Why, it might be asked, was Barnabas thought to be Zeus, the king of the gods? Would we not have expected the people to call Paul, because of his position of leadership, Zeus, and Barnabas, who served as an associate, Hermes? Nevertheless this is not what happened. The Lystrans obviously believed that the greatest deity does not work but is served by lesser gods. Thus the apparently more reticent Barnabas was called Zeus whilst Paul, the apparent spokesman, is identified as Hermes, the messenger of the gods.

Barnabas and Paul, unable to understand the Lycaonian language, innocently observed the great excitement of the crowd. It was only when the priest of the temple of Zeus brought oxen and garlands to the gates, because he and the crowd wanted to offer sacrifices to honour them, that Barnabas and Paul realised what was happening. Immediately they repudiated the blasphemous identification of themselves with gods.

Shortly after this incident, the mission to Lystra came to a sudden end. Some Jews arrived from Pisidian Antioch and Iconium and stirred up the crowd into a murderous mob. Paul was stoned and his body dragged out of the city, apparently dead. He was, however, still alive and the next day departed with Barnabas to Derbe.

Little is said about the mission in Derbe other than that the good news was successfully preached there. Then, in the face of great danger, they more or less retraced their steps to Syrian Antioch, where their journey had begun. On arriving there, after what had been an absence of about two years, they gathered the church together and reported all that had been achieved. They gave God all the honour and the glory and emphasised that *He* had 'opened the door of faith to the Gentiles' (Acts 14:27).

Discussion Starters

1. How can a Christian effectively communicate God's message to a non-believing audience?

_____

_____

_____

_____

_____

2. How did Barnabas and Paul react to being mistaken for gods?

_____

_____

_____

_____

_____

3. Why should we worship only God?

_____

_____

_____

_____

_____

4. In what ways might idolatry affect the lives of people today?

_____

_____

_____

_____

5. Why was Paul the victim of stoning (Acts 14:19) and not Barnabas also?

_____

_____

_____

_____

_____

6. What were the priorities of Barnabas and Paul during their return trip to Syrian Antioch?

_____

_____

_____

_____

_____

7. To whom did Barnabas and Paul give all the honour and glory when speaking about their missionary journey (Acts 14:27; 15:4,12)?

_____

_____

_____

_____

_____

8. Significance is attached to the fact that God had opened the door of faith to the Gentiles (Acts 14:27). Why is this important?

_____

_____

_____

_____

_____

Personal Application

The death of Herod Agrippa I in AD 44 is attributed to the direct intervention of God because he did not reject the divine honours bestowed upon him by the pagan populace nor rebuke them for their flattery (Acts 12:21–23). To be devoured by worms was an extremely painful and shameful death. Unlike Herod, Barnabas and Paul do not succumb to the crowd's adulation but emphasise that they are not gods, but men, and bringers of good news. Glory, majesty, power and authority belong to God alone.

Seeing Jesus in the Scriptures

Many people who had been eager to worship Barnabas and Paul very soon sought vengeance. The sudden, changeable actions of crowds are a well-known fact of life. Jews in the synagogue at Nazareth marvelled at the gracious words which proceeded out of the mouth of Jesus. Yet these same people attempted to throw Him over a cliff (cf Luke 4:22,29). People in Jerusalem shouted 'Hosanna' on Palm Sunday but cried 'Crucify him' a few days later (cf Matt. 21:9; Luke 23:21). The fickle nature of people means that today's heroes can easily become tomorrow's victims of fanatical hatred.

WEEK 6

Facing an Acute Problem

Opening Icebreaker

Discuss what you consider to be the ways in which people might corrupt the truth of the gospel.

Bible Readings

- Acts 15:1–35
- Romans 3:21–31
- Ephesians 2:8–9

Opening Our Eyes

The fact that Gentile converts were readily accepted into fellowship by baptism without circumcision was a serious problem for certain Jews who considered themselves to be God's chosen defenders of the truth. For this reason they considered it necessary to try and nullify the revolutionary teaching of men such as Paul and Barnabas. But what could they do to prevent Christianity becoming a new religion? Some members of the Jerusalem church believed that they knew the answer and were determined to intervene.

Previously the Jerusalem church had appointed Barnabas to assist and encourage the new converts in Antioch to stay true to the Lord (Acts 11:22–23). Now, without any authority to do what they did, some unnamed Jews came from Judea to Antioch and attempted to force their own strict rules and regulations on the Gentiles. What a false and dangerous message it was that they brought! 'Unless you are circumcised, according to the custom taught by Moses, you cannot be saved' (Acts 15:1). Therefore, to become a Christian, a Gentile must first become a Jew.

What was the true relationship of Christianity to Judaism? This was a major theological problem that the Early Christians must face. Had they not done so Christianity would have developed into nothing more than a sect of Judaism! For, by claiming that a Gentile could not be saved unless he was circumcised, the foundations of the Christian faith were being openly challenged. It is not an exaggeration to say that this was a major threat to the future development of Christianity worldwide. Hence, Paul and Barnabas were sent to Jerusalem, accompanied by some other believers, to talk to the apostles and elders about this issue. On their arrival they told the whole church of the signs and wonders God had done among the Gentiles. Even so, some men who had been Pharisees prior to their conversion were immediately antagonistic. They vociferously insisted that all Gentile converts must be circumcised and be required to follow the Law of Moses just as any Jew.

Rather than continue this dispute with the whole assembly, the apostles and elders decided to meet privately with the delegation from Antioch to discuss this issue. A difference of opinion existed even among the leaders but eventually, after a long discussion, Peter stood up and gave his judgment. He was followed by Barnabas and Paul. Noticeably, during this debate, Barnabas returned to a role of prominence (Acts 15:12,25). Presumably this was because he was better known than Paul in the congregation in Jerusalem.

James, who was himself scrupulous in observance of the Law, assumed the responsibility of summing up the debate. Being a strict Jew, would he be biased and side with the party of the Pharisees? Obviously not, for primarily he bases his judgment upon the prophetic word and quotes Amos 9:11–12. He accepts that God had always purposed the salvation of the Gentiles. It was not a divine afterthought that they would share the privileges hitherto restricted to Israel. Hence, James was convinced that the missionary endeavours of Peter, Barnabas and Paul had been greatly used by God for the incorporation of Gentiles into the Church.

Antioch had sent a delegation to Jerusalem, now Jerusalem would return the courtesy. A delegation, with a conciliatory letter, would accompany Barnabas and Paul back to Antioch. The reading of this letter to the Christians in Antioch resulted in great joy. It was now clearly confirmed that God grants salvation by grace alone.

Discussion Starters

1. Why was it a mistake to add circumcision and other legalistic requirements as necessary criteria for salvation?

_____

_____

_____

_____

_____

2. Is it possible for a person to have faith in Jesus *and* to have the law orientation of the Pharisees? Are both ever observed in Christians today?

_____

_____

_____

_____

_____

3. Does the church in Antioch set a good example for dealing with differences of opinion and divisions?

_____

_____

_____

_____

_____

4. What did the speeches of Barnabas and Paul contribute to the Council at Jerusalem?

_____

_____

_____

_____

_____

5. How did the Jerusalem Council members know that their decisions were directed by the Holy Spirit as indicated in this letter (Acts 15:28)?

_____

_____

_____

_____

_____

6. The church in Jerusalem chose delegates and sent them to Antioch with Paul and Barnabas. Why?

_____

_____

_____

_____

_____

7. Does unity mean that everyone must always agree? How do you support your answer?

_____

_____

_____

_____

_____

8. Should true gospel churches work together on matters of common concern? How does this apply in your situation?

_____

_____

_____

_____

_____

Personal Application

James recommended that Gentile converts should not be subject to Jewish regulations. Nevertheless, whilst liberating the Gentiles from such regulations and accepting that salvation is by grace and through faith alone, there are certain things that Gentiles ought to do. In order to respect Jewish Christian convictions they are requested to 'abstain from food sacrificed to idols, from blood, from the meat of strangled animals and from sexual immorality' (Acts 15:29). These were reasonable requests and could, therefore, be accepted. Neither Jewish nor Gentile Christians would reject the first stipulation should it affect their allegiance to Jesus Christ. Nor would they condone sexual immorality. But what about abstaining from things strangled and from blood? These would be courteous concessions to Jewish consciences that would help to establish Christian unity. Likewise, we should be careful not to unnecessarily offend others today – no matter what form this may take providing that it does not cause us to sin in any way.

Seeing Jesus in the Scriptures

Peter reminded the Christians in Jerusalem that he, himself, had shared the gospel with the household of Cornelius several years before (see Acts 11:1–18). At that time God had clearly accepted the Gentiles for they had received the Holy Spirit as had the Jews. Furthermore, Peter echoes the words of Jesus to condemn the impossible legalistic demands that the Pharisees laid on men's shoulders (Matt. 23:4). He reaches the climax of the issue in his conclusion '... that through the grace of the Lord Jesus Christ we shall be saved in the same manner as they (Acts 15:11, NKJV). Both Jew and Gentile alike will be saved by grace.

WEEK 7

Behaviour versus Belief

Opening Icebreaker

Consider how a Christian should respond to criticism. How might we ascertain whether it is constructive or destructive?

Bible Readings

- Acts 15:36–41
- Galatians 2:11–21

Opening Our Eyes

A great attribute of the Bible is that no attempt, whatever, is made to paint an idealised picture of its heroes. Ordinary men and women did extraordinary things because they had faith in a supernatural God, but they were not perfect. They revealed many human weaknesses and experienced both success and failure. Otherwise, their lives would have been inapplicable to ours for they would have set an unattainable standard.

Barnabas and Paul were faithful servants of God but they had their failings as well as their virtues. For instance, Paul suggested to Barnabas that they return to the churches they had established during their previous missionary efforts in Galatia to see how the new believers were progressing. Barnabas willingly agreed, with the proviso that they take his cousin, John Mark, with them as they had done on a previous occasion. Maybe this was to give John Mark another chance to prove himself a worthwhile companion. But Paul adamantly refused this demand and the contention became so sharp between them that they parted company.

The separation of Paul and Barnabas is a distressing incident for it was surely not the work of the Holy Spirit. Neither of the men would give way and so a break in fellowship was inevitable. What was their problem concerning John Mark? Paul objected due to the fact that he had deserted them at Pamphylia during their first missionary journey and had returned to Jerusalem. He had quit before the job was done. Does this not strongly suggest that his commitment as a travelling companion was questionable? Having failed once, at a crucial time, might he not fail again? Despite this possibility Barnabas was willing to reinstate his cousin as a fellow worker. Paul thought otherwise and was not prepared to risk a recurrence.

Possibly you have experienced the frustration of being associated with unreliable people – those who do not do what they have promised. Eventually you learn not to count on them. If there's important work to be done it's natural to turn to someone else who is known to be reliable. Therefore, perhaps you can appreciate and condone Paul's attitude towards John Mark. Or maybe, like Barnabas, you believe that everyone deserves another chance to redeem themselves.

The development of Gentile Christianity owed a tremendous amount to the vision and courage of Barnabas. Hence, it appears strange that there came a time when he followed Peter's example and separated himself from uncircumcised Gentile Christians, and would no longer eat with them. Paul is surprised by behaviour that he considered to be uncharacteristic of Barnabas (Gal. 2:13). This unfortunate incident reveals that even mature Christians are capable of succumbing to the prejudices of their backgrounds.

Although Barnabas, Paul and John Mark had their differences, they were not irreconcilable. They did not entertain any lingering bitterness towards each other. Their example teaches us many important lessons. Clearly it is necessary to be as alert as Paul was in identifying doctrinal threats. At the same time our aim should always be to restore, rather than to condemn, the guilty person or persons. As Christians it is necessary to avoid developing a severely critical attitude which makes no allowance for human weaknesses. The other extreme is to be too soft and so participate in an unacceptable moral alliance. A balanced approach can sometimes be difficult and even the most experienced believers make mistakes.

Discussion Starters

1. Think of some examples from the Bible that reveal how even the most experienced people of God, when left to their own devices, failed.

   _____

   _____

   _____

   _____

   _____

2. Under what circumstances should Christians confront others? Consider Nehemiah 13:11; Matthew 18:15–17; Luke 17:3; Ephesians 5:11.

   _____

   _____

   _____

   _____

   _____

3. How might conflict be resolved?

   _____

   _____

   _____

   _____

4. Paul's letters indicate that he was eventually reconciled to both Barnabas (1 Cor. 9:6) and John Mark (Col. 4:10; 2 Tim. 4:11). Why is it necessary to forgive those who have hurt us?

   _____

   _____

   _____

   _____

5. Barnabas is referred to as an 'apostle' (Acts 14:4,14). What does this mean?

_____

_____

_____

_____

_____

6. Peter, Barnabas and others were not practising what they preached (Gal. 2:11–14). Why did Paul react as he did?

_____

_____

_____

_____

_____

7. How should a Christian respond to failure? Consider Micah 7:8 and Hebrews 13:5b.

_____

_____

_____

_____

_____

8. As we come to the conclusion of our study, what practical and spiritual lessons have you learnt from the life of Barnabas?

_____

_____

_____

_____

_____

Personal Application

No leader can be relied upon to always get it right and so, how can we avoid being led astray? How was it possible for Barnabas, who had been mightily used by God, to withdraw from fellowship with Gentile Christians in Antioch? The root cause of the problem was that Barnabas had momentarily focused his eyes on men and on Peter in particular; instead of on God. Because of this distraction he was not straightforward about the truth of the gospel. We need to constantly keep our eyes upon Jesus.

Seeing Jesus in the Scriptures

The closer we are to God, the greater will be our love for people. All failures in the Christian life are due to looking away from God. Peter walked on the water towards Jesus. But when he looked at the threatening waves he panicked. He forgot that Jesus was only a short distance away. And so, terrified, he began to sink. 'Save me Lord!' he shouted. Instantly Jesus reached out his hand and caught him (Matt. 14:28–31). Since then many Christians have daringly stepped out in faith, confidently expecting to accomplish some great work for God, and been bitterly disappointed. Does this suggest that they are fools to have done so? The answer is no. What we need to remember is that God's great servants of the past sometimes stumbled but they got up again with the help that faith in God always provides.

Leader's Notes

Week 1: Helping the Needy

Opening Icebreaker
The idea of this exercise is to consider the various ways that we can help others both spiritually and physically. Sometimes little things can be a great encouragement.

Aim of the Session
To show that we should give sacrificially, out of a grateful heart, so that God will be glorified.

Discussion Starters
1. The sale of property and subsequent distribution of the proceeds was voluntary. This point is emphasised by Peter who said that Ananias and Sapphira were free to keep their land for themselves or to sell it (Acts 5:4). Mary was the owner of a large residence that appears to have been an important meeting place of many Christians in Jerusalem (Acts 12:12). Apparently the scene portrayed here is one of affluence and as such reveals that not all Christians totally liquidated their assets.

2. Barnabas was a generous man because he was thankful for what God had done for him. Ananias and Sapphira were greedy and dishonest. Their motive was not primarily to help the poor; rather it was to win popularity and gain power. Christians should be seen to be doing things, but not doing things to seek the approval of onlookers (Matt. 6:1).

3. '... I remember you in my prayers night and day ...' (2 Tim. 1:3, NKJV). This must have been a great encouragement to young Timothy to know that Paul

was constantly and specifically praying for him. Think of the impact we might have upon people today by encouraging them to serve God with their lives. An email, a letter or card, a phone call or a visit may be a source of encouragement, especially to someone experiencing difficulties.

4. The Bible never condemns a person for being wealthy; what it does condemn is attaining wealth by ungodliness and the failure to use it for the good of others. Any Christian who is preoccupied with accumulating material possessions and does not develop a habit of generosity falls short of attaining his or her full potential. Greed causes us to think only of ourselves.

5. A casual glance at James would appear to contradict the biblical doctrine of justification by faith. Paul writes that we are saved by faith alone apart from works (Rom. 3; Gal. 2), but James states that faith without works is useless (2:20) and that works are necessary for salvation (2:24). Observe that James is saying not that works must be added to faith in order to be saved, but that works are the visible sign of a living faith. They are proof that faith is genuine.

6. Our spiritual wellbeing depends on good relationships. 'Two are better than one … If one falls down, his friend can help him up … A cord of three strands is not quickly broken (Eccl. 4:9–12). Biblical fellowship is much more than meeting together for Sunday worship; it involves heartfelt commitment by and obligations of Christians to one another, founded on mutual love.

7. Are we sometimes disappointed by the behaviour of our brothers and sisters in Christ? Perhaps a friend says that he or she will visit, but makes no effort to do so. Maybe we do a kind deed for someone and there is no response. Christians should be encouraged by realising what God has done for them. Then they should encourage other believers to grow in their faith.

8. Christian fellowship involves serious commitment to one another, based on practical support, prayer and encouragement to trust unwaveringly in the Lord. Church members are responsible for the spiritual welfare of their brothers and sisters in Christ. They should help any who wander from the truth to be restored as illustrated in James 5:19–20.

Week 2: A True Friend

Opening Icebreaker
To spark ideas amongst the group, read Proverbs 17:17; Colossians 3:13 and 1 Peter 2:17. Consider characteristics such as loyalty, forgiveness, kindness and respect.

Aim of the Session
To show that healthy relationships are an essential element of the Christian life. To have a friend you must be one!

Discussion Starters
1. Saul was responsible for the persecution and death of men and women who claimed to follow Jesus (Acts 22:4). Christians in Jerusalem had not forgotten this and questioned his miraculous conversion. Was he perhaps pretending to be a Christian in order to do more damage? Neither did his former Jewish associates trust him. Such was the hatred of some Greek-speaking Jews, because of his defection, that they made plans to kill him (Acts 9:29).

2. It can be difficult to forgive those who grievously sin against us. However, our unwillingness to forgive others reveals that we have not understood God's forgiveness. Jesus forgave those who crucified Him (Luke 23:34). If we refuse to forgive others our Father will not forgive our sins (Matt. 6:14–15). Forgiveness may not always be

immediate; it can be a process or a journey for the one who has been hurt. Being willing to start the journey is the key. Drawing on God's resources will allow us to become better rather than bitter.

3. Luke does not tell us why Barnabas came to act as intermediary for Saul. Certainly there were similarities between them. They both came from Jewish backgrounds. Furthermore, they spoke Greek as their native tongue which would assist their initial contact. Maybe they had met before this occasion. Some people are of the opinion that they had been students together at the university in Tarsus years earlier. Such reasoning is speculative. If they had been friends, or even acquaintances, we would have expected Saul to have immediately contacted Barnabas when he arrived in Jerusalem.

4. An example of friendship in the Old Testament is the deep relationship between Jonathan and David. '... Jonathan made a covenant with David because he loved him as himself' (1 Sam. 18:3). This despite the fact that David had been anointed to be the next king, a position that by birthright belonged to Jonathan. The New Testament also reveals that God is our constant friend and will never leave us (Heb. 13:5).

5. Barnabas vouched for Saul based upon his belief that it was the will of God. Saul's actions were also convincing (Acts 9:20). Thus Barnabas reached out in love and readily accepted Saul as a brother in Christ. Christians must avoid recklessness but there are situations where they must take a calculated risk and step out in faith. The only act more risky than trusting God is not trusting Him.

6. Barnabas passionately believed that those who did wrong deserved another chance. That is why he did not reject Saul or John Mark, despite their previous record, but rightly recognised their great potential. How often do we

give others the benefit of the doubt? The Lord taught us to pray, 'Forgive us our sins, for we also forgive everyone who sins against us' (Luke 11:4).

7. The teachings of Jesus about our forgiveness of others are brief in comparison to our need of God's forgiveness. Nevertheless, we are left in no doubt that the spirit of genuine forgiveness recognises no boundaries. When Peter asked how often he must forgive his brother, Jesus insists: 'I do not say to you, up to seven times, but up to seventy times seven' (Matt. 18:22, NKJV). That was tantamount to saying that forgiveness cannot be described quantitatively but only qualitatively. As God forgives us without limit, we must forgive those who have sinned against us.

8. Barnabas, and earlier Ananias (Acts 9:10–19), enabled Saul to become established within the Christian community. Had they not done so, he may never have become the blessing to us that he became. Do we give people another chance, irrespective of any previous failings, and urge them to fully develop their God-given gifts?

Week 3: Full of the Holy Spirit and Strong in Faith

Opening Icebreaker
The idea of this exercise is for the group to appreciate what a great privilege it is for Christians to have God's Spirit dwelling within them. Consider how we might grieve the Holy Spirit of God (Eph. 4:30–32), or quench the Spirit's fire (1 Thess. 5:19).

Aim of the Session
To show that the Holy Spirit empowers us to achieve what

we could never accomplish by ourselves.

Discussion Starters

1. Rapid numerical growth due to new converts, although something to be welcomed, can create practical problems. People can unintentionally be overlooked, thus causing a division within the fellowship. Consider Acts 6:1–8. Delegation enables leaders not to be over-burdened and also avoids others being under-utilised. Sometimes it may be necessary to seek help from elsewhere (Acts 11:25).

2. As a Greek-speaking Jewish Christian, and a native of Cyprus, Barnabas was a wise choice for the task at Antioch. His qualifications were excellent: (1) a good man; (2) full of the Holy Spirit; (3) full of faith. As a result 'a great number of people were brought to the Lord' (Acts 11:24).

3. The Antioch church rightly admitted both Jews and Gentiles without distinction. No one is ever banished from the presence of the love of God because of their nationality, background or social status. All that is necessary to be forever free from God's condemnation is faith in Jesus Christ. 'For there is no distinction between Jew and Greek, for the same Lord over all is rich to all who call upon Him' (Rom. 10:12, NKJV).

4. Babes in Christ are like young plants. In order to thrive they need regular attention. They need feeding when they are hungry. After the initial excitement of believing, Christians can experience doubts. Satan will attack them. For these reasons Barnabas repeatedly encouraged the believers in Antioch to trust unwaveringly in the Lord.

5. Satan's strategy is the same today as it was in the Garden of Eden (Gen. 3:1). He questions the truthfulness of God's Word and then subtly tries to distort it. That is why we live in an age where there is a plethora of

aberrant beliefs and without the power of the Holy Spirit our hearts and minds will be oblivious to the truth. We can resist temptation, as Jesus did, with 'the sword of the Spirit, which is the word of God' (Eph. 6:17; Matt. 4:1–11).

6. The Holy Spirit exists eternally in perfect union with the Father and the Son. He is the One sent to us by the Father and the Son to be our Helper (John 14:16–17). Without the power of the Holy Spirit we can accomplish nothing of any lasting value.

7. Undoubtedly the most important thing in the life of any Christian is to be filled with the Holy Spirit. We are dependent on Him for convicting us of sin. He transforms our lives. Anyone who is filled with the Holy Spirit will manifest the characteristics listed in Galatians 5:22–23.

8. The Christians in Jerusalem faced a wave of persecution soon after the martyrdom of Stephen. This resulted in them being scattered throughout the neighbouring regions. How did they react? These believers had lost many things, but not their faith in what had been accomplished. Death had been unable to defeat Jesus. He was alive and He was their Lord. They spoke enthusiastically about what they had seen and heard. Hence, the good news of salvation was spread wherever they went. Faith in God can accomplish wonders.

Week 4: Ministering Together

Opening Icebreaker
Consider advantages such as mutual support, a greater range of gifts, accountability and a counterbalancing of extremes. Teamwork also provides the opportunity to train inexperienced men and women.

Aim of the Session

To show that partnership with those who love God is an essential part of what it means to be a Christian.

Discussion Starters

1. God takes a person at their own estimate of themselves, reverses it, and acts accordingly. Mary in her song of praise reminds us that, 'He has brought down rulers from their thrones but has lifted up the humble. He has filled the hungry with good things but has sent the rich away empty' (Luke 1:52–53). We remain humble by recognising who we are and who God is.

2. Wealth and power are accepted standards of greatness. Jesus, however, radically reverses this assumption and says that true greatness is to respond to the needs of those around us. He sets the example for us to follow (Mark 10:45).

3. The Christians in Antioch sent relief to their brothers and sisters in Judea; everyone voluntarily giving as much as possible. Generosity should be an obvious characteristic of the family of God because it demonstrates that He is first in our lives. '… God loves a cheerful giver' (2 Cor. 9:7).

4. It was inconceivable to the church in Antioch that they should not help the Christians in Judea during their time of desperate need. They had a width of vision that saw way beyond their local situation. Primarily they were concerned about building God's kingdom rather than their own empire. Therefore they did not isolate themselves from the needs of other churches.

5. The development of Gentile Christianity owed a tremendous amount to the vision and courage of Barnabas. He had been instrumental in enabling Saul to develop his ministry (Acts 9:27; 11:25). Barnabas was an effective leader of the church in Antioch. He and Saul made a physically demanding and dangerous missionary

journey to Cyprus and Pamphylia, Pisidia, Lycaonia and back to Antioch (Acts 13:4–14:28).

6. In Paphos it was Paul, not Barnabas, who would be the leader. The expedition is now referred to as 'Paul and his companions' (Acts 13:13). It does not appear that Barnabas encountered any difficulty in falling into second place. Whenever he saw the grace of God actively working in the lives of fellow Christians his heart was filled with joy. Jesus tells us to celebrate the success of His people rather than compete against them (Mark 9:38–40).

7. Barnabas and Saul did not decide to leave Antioch and then ask for prayer. It was the church, under the guidance of the Holy Spirit, who commissioned them for this work to which they were called. After they had fasted and prayed, the church members laid hands on them and sent them off on the first momentous missionary tour to the Gentile world (Acts 13:3). Likewise, today it is the duty of every local church to be receptive to the Holy Spirit so as to discern whom He may be gifting and calling.

8. The Holy Spirit graciously allocates to every Christian a gift or gifts which are to be used for the glory of God. These gifts are to be used within the Christian community and for the common good of humanity whenever possible. Christians have a duty to recognise and help fellow believers develop their God-given gifts. Are we, like Barnabas, willing to work for the success of others?

Week 5: To God be the Glory

Opening Icebreaker
The idea of this exercise is to emphasise that our love of God must express itself in deeds. This is made abundantly clear by Jesus (Matt. 22:34–40).

Aim of the Session

It is vital for us to realise that God alone is worthy of worship.

Discussion Starters

1. Acts 14:15–17 provides us with a brief sermon preached to a pagan crowd. Unlike the Jews or Gentiles who attended the synagogue worship they are unacquainted with the God of Israel or with any of the Hebrew prophets. It would, therefore, be pointless to refer directly to the Old Testament Scriptures. Hence, Barnabas and Paul speak about the living God. The evidence can be seen. Who do the people think made heaven and earth and everything in them? If the good news of Jesus Christ is to be effectively proclaimed we must use language that people can understand.

2. In typical Eastern gesture Barnabas and Saul tore their clothes as a sign of horror and ran in among the multitude, crying out: 'Men, why are you doing this? We too are only men, human like you' (Acts 14:14–15; see also Acts 10:25–26). Such immediate action clearly repudiates the hero worship of a person.

3. As God's servants we know that He created people to worship Him and Him alone. We know that God is a jealous God (Exod. 34:14). He does not permit anyone to take His place. God wants an intimate relationship with all His people and is intolerant of anything or anyone who interferes.

4. An idol, whether it is a physical object or simply an idea, is anything that takes precedence in a person's life instead of the true and living God (Deut. 5:7–9; see also Col. 1:18). Undoubtedly the greatest idol in the heart of us all is the one called 'self'. Today, the only acceptable image of God is Jesus Christ (Heb. 1:3).

5. It is impossible for us to say why Paul alone became

the victim of stoning and not Barnabas also. It might be argued that Paul being instrumental in the healing of the man meant that he was the prime target of their fury. Even so, it is unlikely that Barnabas would have escaped a similar injustice and so we can only assume that he could not be found. Certainly in Iconium the plan had been to stone both Paul and Barnabas (Acts 14:5).

6. The obvious route from Derbe to Syrian Antioch would have been via Tarsus. However, irrespective of the danger, Barnabas and Paul returned to the Galatian cities of Lystra, followed by Iconium and then Pisidian Antioch. The young converts in these places were exposed to many dangers and so it was important that they were further instructed in the truths of the gospel. Any evangelism that places all the emphasis upon conversions has lost sight of this. Besides encouraging the disciples in these churches to continue in the faith, they also appointed elders for them and with prayer and fasting committed them to the Lord, in whom they had come to trust.

7. All that was said by Barnabas and Paul glorified God alone. It was not about what these intrepid missionaries had achieved, nor their sufferings. Rather, it was about all the great things God had enabled them to do.

8. The missionary journey of Barnabas and Paul was not the beginning of the conversion of the Gentiles. Nevertheless, it was the first major and deliberate advance into the Gentile world. Now churches which either predominantly or totally consisted of non-Jews were established.

Week 6: Facing an Acute Problem

Opening Icebreaker
The aim of this exercise is to stress the need to oppose false

teaching. Anyone who teaches that parts of the Bible are irrelevant, that it needs to be added to, or quotes sections of it out of context, needs to be corrected. Self-willed opinions that are in opposition to biblical truth frequently lead to the formation of groups masquerading as Christianity.

Aim of the Session

To show that through faith in Christ alone we are made right with God.

Discussion Starters

1. Certain Jews sincerely believed that salvation was through Jesus plus circumcision and obeying the Law of Moses. Thus it was to reject those whom God had accepted. Christianity was in danger of becoming a sect of Judaism. That is why Barnabas and Paul argued forcefully, and at great length, against these false teachers. They stressed that only faith in Jesus Christ is obligatory for salvation.

2. Today there are those who claim that faith in Jesus Christ alone is insufficient for salvation. They stress the need for works or religious observances in order to be saved. This, despite the fact that salvation is never a reward for the good things we have done so that none of us can boast about it (Eph. 2:8–9). Only through the grace of the Lord Jesus Christ is anyone saved from eternal condemnation.

3. The circumcision controversy had arisen because of men from Jerusalem and so it was appropriate that the two churches most immediately involved sought, sooner rather than later, a sensible solution that would enable Jewish and Gentile Christians to unite. A special meeting was held in Jerusalem to discuss the matter and, after much debate, a solution in accordance with the Word of God was agreed (Acts 15:15–18).

4. Barnabas and Paul wisely refrained from mentioning circumcision for that would have been counterproductive. Anger would only have resulted in more conflict. Instead they concentrated their argument upon what God had done through them among the Gentiles. The Holy Spirit had witnessed to their work in Galatia as manifestly as to Peter's work in Caesarea. Was this not incontrovertible evidence that their missionary endeavours had God's seal of approval!

5. The Early Christians, despite their failings, were mightily blessed by the power of the Holy Spirit. They were aware of His presence to guide and direct them. The letter sent by the church in Jerusalem to Antioch is an example of this. Unanimously they had agreed what to write. Spirit-filled people are aware of His presence because of the harmony which prevails.

6. The church in Jerusalem courteously sent a conciliatory letter, entrusted to Judas and Silas, who travelled to Antioch with Barnabas and Paul. Sending Judas and Silas was a sign of friendship and would achieve far more than just sending an official letter. Furthermore, these men could clarify orally any queries that might arise. They stayed in Antioch for a while and spoke extensively to the Christians, encouraging them and strengthening their faith.

7. It is important for us to realise that unity and uniformity are not identical. Christians differ from one another in culture, education, personality and many other ways. Unity has always been difficult for Christians to achieve because of their various ideas about what is important. Despite their many differences Christians are united in that they believe in one God, Father, Son and Holy Spirit (Eph. 4:4–6).

8. True gospel churches have a responsibility to manifest their spiritual unity in Christ by working together on matters of common concern (Acts 15:1–31; Rom. 15:26). Truth, however, must never be sacrificed for the sake of

unity (2 Cor. 6:14–16). Consider your attitude to working with other denominations and groups.

Week 7: Behaviour versus Belief

Opening Icebreaker
The purpose of this exercise is to differentiate between positive and negative criticism. Is it intended to hurt or to heal?

Aim of the Session
To show that many believers fail not at the beginning of their walk with God but after many years of faithful service.

Discussion Starters
1. Moses (Exod. 2:11–12); David (2 Sam. 11:1–5) and Elijah (1 Kings 19:3) were very familiar with the ways of God when they made their greatest mistakes. Barnabas and Peter were experienced Christian leaders when they erred; a time when we would have least expected them to do so. The failures of these servants of God are stern warnings of the need to be constantly alert against the spiritual forces of evil.

2. To see Paul and Peter, two leading apostles of Jesus Christ, in a public confrontation is significant. That is why God tells us about it. God wants us to realise that arguments are sometimes regrettably necessary for there are fundamental issues to resolve without which you sacrifice Christian truths. Despite this there is a tendency today to avoid any form of confrontation for fear that it might cause offence. This is a mistake, for all Christians have a duty to challenge inappropriate behaviour.

3. Peace at any price is not what the Bible teaches (Rom. 12:18). We should, however, make every effort to

avoid conflict. Abram gave Lot first choice of grazing lands, putting peace before preference (Gen. 13:7–9). Isaac moved to other locations so as to maintain peace (Gen. 26:12–22).

4. Some people believe that the quarrel between Barnabas and Paul had a good result, namely: that God's providence overruled and created two missionary teams instead of one. Such an outcome should never be used to justify Christians quarrelling. This unpleasant incident was due to a collision of personalities and was not sanctioned by God. Unity should never be promoted at the expense of truth; but neither should our own personal agenda be allowed to cause division. Consider Matthew 6:14–15; Luke 17:3–4 and Colossians 3:13.

5. The word 'apostles' is attributed to those personally chosen by Christ. It included the Twelve, Matthias who succeeded Judas Iscariot, and Paul. Although Paul did not fulfil all of the requirements recorded in Acts 1:21–22, he knew that God had directly called him to be an apostle to the Gentiles. The title can also be used in a wider sense. For example, Epaphroditus was an apostle (messenger) of the Philippian church (Phil. 2:25). Likewise, Barnabas was an apostle (messenger) sent out by the Syrian Antioch church.

6. Peter knew in his heart that he was wrong to isolate himself from Gentile Christians. In spite of that he acted against his better judgment and thus gave a wrong impression. Paul, therefore, did not hesitate to publicly oppose Peter to his face because he was clearly in the wrong and had led others, even staunch Barnabas, into joining him in playing the hypocrite. Christian leadership involves great responsibility towards others.

7. What do we mean by failure? Is the failure due to our mistake, or beyond our control? Is it the result of

a deliberate or unintentional act? We all fail and need to turn to God in repentance and trust. Those who persevere will be rewarded.

8. Barnabas was a good man, full of the Holy Spirit and of faith. Hence, he actively served God. Action always involves the exertion of energy and so many people, who have intentions of doing something good, fail to do it. Evil triumphs when good people do nothing. Give everyone in the group the opportunity to ask questions they still might have about Barnabas. How might we effectively serve God?

Latest Resources

The Popular *Cover to Cover* Bible Study Series

1 Corinthians
Growing a Spirit-filled church
ISBN: 978-1-85345-374-8

2 Corinthians
Restoring harmony
ISBN: 978-1-85345-551-3

1,2,3 John
Walking in the truth
ISBN: 978-1-78259-763-6

1 Peter
Good reasons for hope
ISBN: 978-1-78259-088-0

2 Peter
Living in the light of God's promises
ISBN: 978-1-78259-403-1

1 Timothy
Healthy churches –
effective Christians
ISBN: 978-1-85345-291-8

23rd Psalm
The Lord is my shepherd
ISBN: 978-1-85345-449-3

2 Timothy and Titus
Vital Christianity
ISBN: 978-1-85345-338-0

Abraham
Adventures of faith
ISBN: 978-1-78259-089-7

Acts 1–12
Church on the move
ISBN: 978-1-85345-574-2

Acts 13–28
To the ends of the earth
ISBN: 978-1-85345-592-6

Barnabas
Son of encouragement
ISBN: 978-1-85345-911-5

Bible Genres
Hearing what the Bible really says
ISBN: 978-1-85345-987-0

Daniel
Living boldly for God
ISBN: 978-1-85345-986-3

David
A man after God's own heart
ISBN: 978-1-78259-444-4

Ecclesiastes
Hard questions and
spiritual answers
ISBN: 978-1-85345-371-7

Elijah
A man and his God
ISBN: 978-1-85345-575-9

Elisha
A lesson in faithfulness
ISBN: 978-1-78259-494-9

Ephesians
Claiming your inheritance
ISBN: 978-1-85345-229-1

Esther
For such a time as this
ISBN: 978-1-85345-511-7

Fruit of the Spirit
Growing more like Jesus
ISBN: 978-1-85345-375-5

Galatians
Freedom in Christ
ISBN: 978-1-85345-648-0

God's Rescue Plan
Finding God's fingerprints
on human history
ISBN: 978-1-85345-294-9

Great Prayers of the Bible
Applying them to our lives today
ISBN: 978-1-85345-253-6

Haggai
Motivating God's people
ISBN: 978-1-78259-686-8

Hebrews
Jesus – simply the best
ISBN: 978-1-85345-337-3

Hosea
The love that never fails
ISBN: 978-1-85345-290-1

Isaiah 1–39
Prophet to the nations
ISBN: 978-1-85345-510-0

Isaiah 40–66
Prophet of restoration
ISBN: 978-1-85345-550-6

Jacob
Taking hold of God's blessing
ISBN: 978-1-78259-685-1

James
Faith in action
ISBN: 978-1-85345-293-2

Jeremiah
The passionate prophet
ISBN: 978-1-85345-372-4

John's Gospel
Exploring the seven miraculous signs
ISBN: 978-1-85345-295-6

Jonah
Rescued from the depths
ISBN: 978-1-78259-762-9

Joseph
The power of forgiveness and reconciliation
ISBN: 978-1-85345-252-9

Joshua 1–10
Hand in hand with God
ISBN: 978-1-85345-542-7

Judges 1–8
The spiral of faith
ISBN: 978-1-85345-681-7

Judges 9–21
Learning to live God's way
ISBN: 978-1-85345-910-8

Luke
A prescription for living
ISBN: 978-1-78259-270-9

Mark
Life as it is meant to be lived
ISBN: 978-1-85345-233-8

Mary
The mother of Jesus
ISBN: 978-1-78259-402-4

Moses
Face to face with God
ISBN: 978-1-85345-336-6

Names of God
Exploring the depths of God's character
ISBN: 978-1-85345-680-0

Nehemiah
Principles for life
ISBN: 978-1-85345-335-9

Parables
Communicating God on earth
ISBN: 978-1-85345-340-3

Philemon
From slavery to freedom
ISBN: 978-1-85345-453-0

Philippians
Living for the sake of the gospel
ISBN: 978-1-85345-421-9

Prayers of Jesus
Hearing His heartbeat
ISBN: 978-1-85345-647-3

Proverbs
Living a life of wisdom
ISBN: 978-1-85345-373-1

Revelation 1–3
Christ's call to the Church
ISBN: 978-1-85345-461-5

Revelation 4–22
The Lamb wins! Christ's final victory
ISBN: 978-1-85345-411-0

Rivers of Justice
Responding to God's call to righteousness today
ISBN: 978-1-85345-339-7

Ruth
Loving kindness in action
ISBN: 978-1-85345-231-4

The Armour of God
Living in His strength
ISBN: 978-1-78259-583-0

The Beatitudes
Immersed in the grace of Christ
ISBN: 978-1-78259-495-6

The Covenants
God's promises and their relevance today
ISBN: 978-1-85345-255-0

The Creed
Belief in action
SBN: 978-1-78259-202-0

The Divine Blueprint
God's extraordinary power in ordinary lives
ISBN: 978-1-85345-292-5

The Holy Spirit
Understanding and experiencing Him
ISBN: 978-1-85345-254-3

The Image of God
His attributes and character
ISBN: 978-1-85345-228-4

The Kingdom
Studies from Matthew's Gospel
ISBN: 978-1-85345-251-2

The Letter to the Colossians
In Christ alone
ISBN: 978-1-855345-405-9

The Letter to the Romans
Good news for everyone
ISBN: 978-1-85345-250-5

The Lord's Prayer
Praying Jesus' way
ISBN: 978-1-85345-460-8

The Prodigal Son
Amazing grace
ISBN: 978-1-85345-412-7

The Second Coming
Living in the light of Jesus' return
ISBN: 978-1-85345-422-6

The Sermon on the Mount
Life within the new covenant
ISBN: 978-1-85345-370-0

Thessalonians
Building Church in changing times
ISBN: 978-1-78259-443-7

The Ten Commandments
Living God's Way
ISBN: 978-1-85345-593-3

The Uniqueness of our Faith
What makes Christianity distinctive?
ISBN: 978-1-85345-232-1

For current prices or to order, visit **www.cwr.org.uk/shop**
Available online or from Christian bookshops.

Be inspired by God.
Every day.

Confidently face life's challenges by equipping yourself daily with God's Word. There is something for everyone...

Every Day with Jesus

Selwyn Hughes' renowned writing is updated by Mick Brooks into these trusted and popular notes.

Life Every Day

Jeff Lucas helps apply the Bible to daily life through his trademark humour and insight.

Inspiring Women
Every Day

Encouragement, uplifting scriptures and insightful daily thoughts for women.

The Manual

Straight-talking guide to help men walk daily with God. Written by Carl Beech. Not available via subscription.

To find out more about all our daily Bible reading notes, visit www.cwr.org.uk/bible-reading-notes or call 01252 784700
Also available in Christian bookshops

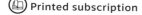 Printed subscription  Large print subscription

 Email subscription Ebook subscription

SmallGroup central

All of our small group ideas and resources in one place

Online:

www.smallgroupcentral.org.uk
is filled with free video teaching,
tools, articles and a whole host
of ideas.

On the road:

A range of seminars themed for
small groups can be brought to
your local community. Contact us at
hello@smallgroupcentral.org.uk

In print:

Books, study guides and DVDs
covering an extensive list of themes,
Bible books and life issues.

Find out more at:
www.smallgroupcentral.org.uk

Courses and events

Waverley Abbey College

Publishing and media

Conference facilities

Transforming lives

CWR's vision is to enable people to experience personal transformation through applying God's Word to their lives and relationships.

Our Bible-based training and resources help people around the world to:
• Grow in their walk with God
• Understand and apply Scripture to their lives
• Resource themselves and their church
• Develop pastoral care and counselling skills
• Train for leadership
• Strengthen relationships, marriage and family life and much more.

Our insightful writers provide daily Bible reading notes and other resources for all ages, and our experienced course designers and presenters have gained an international reputation for excellence and effectiveness.

CWR's Training and Conference Centres in Surrey and East Sussex, England, provide excellent facilities in idyllic settings – ideal for both learning and spiritual refreshment.

CWR Applying God's Word
to everyday life and relationships

CWR, Waverley Abbey House,
Waverley Lane, Farnham,
Surrey GU9 8EP, UK

Telephone: **+44 (0)1252 784700**
Email: **info@cwr.org.uk**
Website: **www.cwr.org.uk**

Registered Charity No. 294387
Company Registration No. 1990308